E.M.E.S.
WALKER HOUSE
RADBROOK COLLEGE
RADBROOK ROAD
SHREWSBURY
SY3 9BJ

SMDS
MADELEY COURT SCHOOL
COURT STREET, MADELEY
TELFORD TF7 5DZ
Telephone: 585704

The **BEANS** series

People at work

Bakery
Carpenter
Fairground Family
Fishing Boat
Garage
Lorry Driver
Oil Rig Worker
Pottery
The Vet

History

The Blacksmith's House
Jubilee Terrace
Vikings

Geography

Aboriginal Family
Apache Family
Arab Village
Boy in Bangladesh
Brazilian Family
Chinnoda's School in India
Chun Ling in China
Eskimo Boy
French Family
German Family
Jamaican Village
KwaZulu, South Africa
Mexico
Moroccan Family
New York Family
Pakistani Village
Sakina in India
Sri Lanka
Village in Egypt
Yik Ming in Hong Kong
Zambia

Browne, Rollo
　Aboriginal family. – (Beans)
　1. Australian aborigines – Australia – Northern Territory – Social life and customs – Juvenile literature
　I. Title　　II. Series
　994.29'0049915　　GN667.N95

ISBN 0-7136-2293-8

A&C Black (Publishers) Limited
35 Bedford Row, London WC1R 4JH

© 1983 A&C Black (Publishers) Limited
First published 1983
Reprinted 1985
Acknowledgments
The map is by Tony Garret
The photograph at the top of pages 12/13 is by Chris Walton
All rights reserved. No part of this publication may be reproduced, stored in a retrieval system, or transmitted in any form or by any means, electronic, mechanical, photocopying, recording or otherwise, without the prior permission of A&C Black (Publishers) Limited.

Filmset by August Filmsetting, Haydock, St. Helens.
Colour reproduction by Hongkong Graphic Arts Service Centre
Printed in Belgium by Brepols S.A., Turnhout

Aboriginal Family

Rollo Browne

Photographs by Chris Fairclough

Adam and Charles Black · London

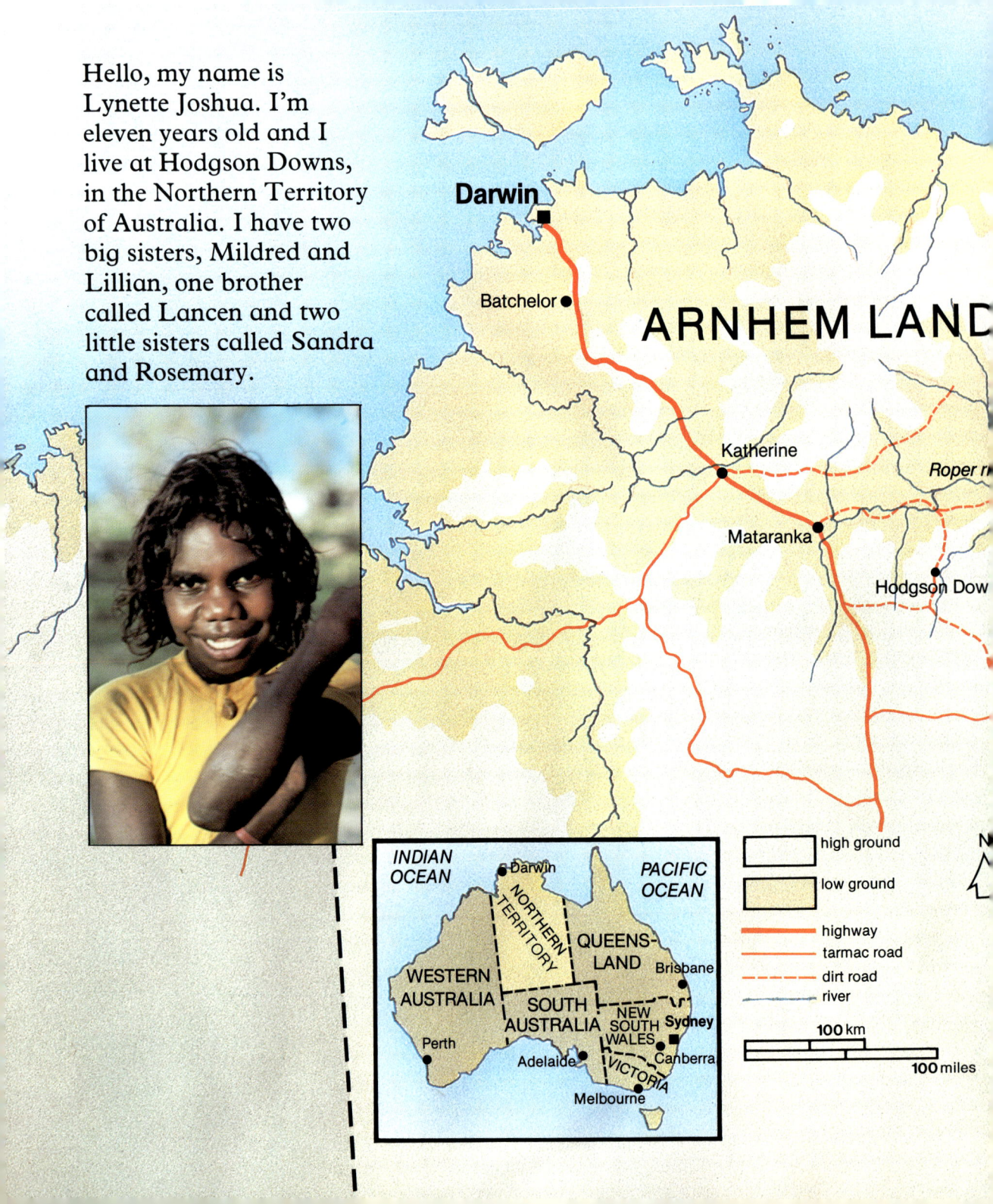

Hello, my name is Lynette Joshua. I'm eleven years old and I live at Hodgson Downs, in the Northern Territory of Australia. I have two big sisters, Mildred and Lillian, one brother called Lancen and two little sisters called Sandra and Rosemary.

We live with our parents at the Camp on Hodgson Downs Cattle Station. The Station used to be a big cattle farm. Now, the farm has been closed down.

Our Camp is called Minyerri. It's named after the big billabong (waterhole) near the Camp. We call it the 'Camp' because Aboriginal people camped there when the cattle station was first started, in 1885.

Hodgson Downs is about 600 kilometres from Darwin, the capital of the Northern Territory. It's a long journey from Darwin to Hodgson Downs. You can take the bus to Mataranka, our nearest town. Mataranka is about 160 kilometres from the Camp. Then you'd have to wait for a lift to Minyerri. Buses don't come out to Hodgson Downs. They keep to the main road.

You can't ring us up, but we can get messages on our new two-way radio. Every morning, at seven thirty, my father Leslie turns on the radio. We listen for our call. 'Victor Mike eight Lima Lima, Minyerri Community come in please.' That's Outpost Radio in Darwin calling us.

My father says it's good to have a radio. During the Wet Season, it rains a lot and the roads are often flooded. Then the radio is the only way we can get help or send messages. The Wet Season starts at Christmas time and lasts for about four months. Then the Dry Season begins. There is no rain during the Dry Season. The rivers stop running and dry up into billabongs.

About eighty people live in our Camp. We have over fifteen houses, a big store shed, a meeting shed, a clinic and a shower block.

My family lives in a house built from timber, corrugated iron and concrete. All the houses in the Camp are like ours. Most of the houses have one room with a veranda at the front. We spend most of our time outside on the shady veranda, or down by the billabong.

My mother, Susan, does all the cooking outside. We get up early every morning and mum makes tea and damper for breakfast.

We all know how to make damper. You mix flour, baking powder, salt and water into a smooth dough. Then you pat the dough into little round flat cakes. The dampers are put into the fire and covered with hot ashes. After a little while, they are cooked. They will rise a bit and should have a good crust. I like damper with treacle the best.

Sometimes, mum makes bread in a proper camp oven. This is a big iron pot that sits in the fire. It has a special lid that you cover with hot coals. The bread tastes good but it takes a long time to make.

Mum does most of the cooking and all the cleaning. I often help her when I'm not at school. We do the washing at the tap outside the house, or down at the billabong. All the water which we use for washing and drinking is pumped from the billabong.

I help look after my little sisters, too. The older children always help to look after the younger ones, especially around the Camp.

After breakfast, my mum sends us off to school. Rosemary stays at home. She's too young to go to school. When we've gone, mum collects the firewood or does some washing. Sometimes she goes down to the billabong to look for wild foods. When she's not busy she likes to play cards or talk to friends and relations.

Sandra, Mildred, Lancen and I go to Minyerri School. The school is held in two caravans near the Camp.

There are only two classes in the school. I'm in the Primary class, which we call the Golden Eagles. Sandra is in the Infants class. We call them the Peewees, after the noisy little black and white birds which live around here.

We have two teachers. They live in a caravan near the school. There's an Aboriginal Assistant Teacher, too. She lives in the Camp. She usually teaches the little children who don't speak much English.

Most of the people in the Camp belong to the Alawa tribe. Alawa is the language of the old people in this area. Not many of the children speak Alawa, but I can understand the old people when they talk and tell stories. Most families speak Aboriginal English (Kriol) to each other.

At school we learn English, Maths and other European subjects. Sometimes, one of the older people in the Camp comes to the school to give Alawa lessons. Usually we learn Alawa from our relations at the Camp.

We don't have electricity at the Camp. There is an electricity generator at the school, so we go there to watch films. The films are shown against the wall of the caravan. It's lovely and cool at night, sitting outside and watching a film. There is a trampoline at the school, too, and all the children argue for turns.

The men from our Camp used to work for the Cattle Station. Now that Hodgson Downs Station has closed down, there is no work for any of the men. They have to try and make money in other ways.

Some of the men sell boomerangs. My Uncle Ashwood makes didjeridoos and sells them to shops in the towns. A didjeridoo is a long hollowed out branch of a tree. You blow into it and it makes a low droning sound.

The men play didjeridoos and clap boomerangs together to make corroboree music. Corroboree is when we have dancing and singing for fun. Sometimes, the dancers paint themselves with white clay. It isn't like a rock and roll dance because the men and women always dance separately.

Before the whiteman (mununga) came, the country around here belonged to the Alawa. My granny tells me lots of stories about our country. She says the country was made during the *Dreamtime*. It was made by spirits who travelled across the land.

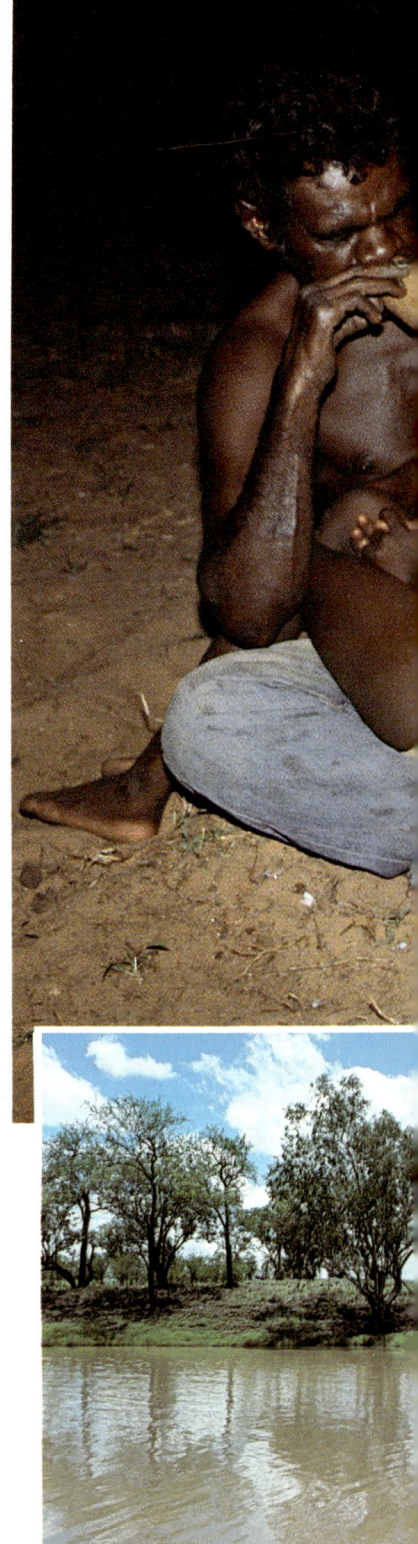

Granny says the Minyerri billabong was made by Wadjurndu, the Goanna Spirit. This is why we say that the billabong is part of the Goanna Dreaming. No-one is allowed to fire a rifle into the water. As long as anyone can remember, the billabong has never dried up. People at the Camp still stay here so they can be close to their country and look after *dreaming places* like the billabong.

11

At the end of the Dry Season, it is *ceremony* time. The radio is used to call people for ceremonies. A lot of people come to join in. Like some of you might go to church, Aborigines go to ceremonies to renew their links with the *Dreamtime spirits* who made the land. We call this our *dreaming*.

Some ceremonies are secret and religious. They are often for men or for women only. At other times, anyone can join in.

At ceremony time, you see all the people who share your dreaming and your *skin group*. People are linked to their land through their dreaming. They are linked to each other through skin groups. All Alawa people belong to a skin group.

We have eight different skin groups. Each skin group has one name for women and another for men.

Your skin name depends on your mother's skin name. My mother's skin name is Nangari, so my sisters and I are Nangala skin and my brother is Jangala skin. Even the little children know their skin names.

People in all the skin groups are like part of your family, even though you might not be related. I call all the women in my mother's skin group, 'mother' and all the men in my father's skin group, 'father'. This is how Aborigines in the Northern Territory are related to each other.

Two years ago, my dad took a job as Assistant Teacher at our school in Minyerri. Dad says that lots of communities want to have Aboriginal teachers in their schools. He went to train at the Aboriginal Teacher Education College, in Batchelor. Batchelor is a town 100 kilometres from Darwin. It's a long way from Hodgson Downs, so dad took the whole family with him.

We lived in a new house near the college. The house had a modern kitchen with an electric stove and a refrigerator.

There was an inside toilet and you even had your own bed. We used to eat in the college canteen, or buy food from the shop and cook at home. The college had a television room, too, and they sometimes held dances.

While dad was working, I went to Batchelor School. It was much bigger than our school at Minyerri. They had a playground with two trampolines. There were some other Aboriginal children at the school. They were mostly the children of people at the college.

At weekends, we sometimes went shopping in Darwin. We always found something to buy, especially cheap clothes. Mildred and I used to watch all the cars and look out for fruit and ice-cream shops.

In the middle of the Dry Season, dad finished his training. We went home to Hodgson Downs and dad was chosen to be president of Minyerri Camp.

Now that dad is president, he has to order food for the Camp. The food is sent from Katherine, a town about 260 kilometres away. Dad orders all the food by radio. Before we had a radio, the food sometimes ran out and we had to go hungry until a message could reach Katherine. Now it's much quicker.

In the Dry Season, a truck brings supplies from Katherine every two weeks. When the truck arrives, dad has to share out all the food. Most people in the camp help to pay for the supplies. We order flour, sugar, tea, salt, baking powder, milk powder and tins of fruit or meat. The truck also brings supplies such as matches, tobacco and bullets.

In the Wet Season, when the roads are blocked, dad orders enough food to last for four months. Once, the truck couldn't cross one of the streams. The driver had to turn around and leave everything in Roper Valley, 45 kilometres away from Minyerri. Some of the men took the new camp tractor to fetch the supplies. They brought everything back on the trailer and stacked it in the store shed.

We don't need to order all our food from Katherine. People collect a lot of food from the countryside (bush) around our Camp. We call this food bush-tucker.

The men often go out hunting for kangaroo, turkey or goanna (big lizards). They take rifles or shotguns if they can. Otherwise they use spears.

Cattle still live on the land around the Station. Some of them are real wild and have never been branded. They are called 'cleanskins'. Every two weeks, a bullock is killed and the meat is shared by everyone in the Camp. We call it the 'killer'.

The men go out early in the morning for the killer. They ride on the back of a truck and take a rifle, butchering knives and an axe. They bring all the meat back to the Camp to share out. We don't waste any of the meat from the killer.

My favourite is rib bones cooked in the fire. If there is enough meat left over, we rub coarse salt into it and hang it up to dry. Then we can store the meat to eat later.

In the Dry Season, there are fish in the streams and waterholes. We catch fish like bream, catfish and barramundi. Barramundi are big fish. Just one of them makes a meal for our whole family. There are turtles and crocodiles, too – not the big saltwater crocodiles, only the little freshwater ones. We catch the turtles and crocodiles with fishing hooks and bait. Turtle meat is very sweet.

I go out hunting for goanna with my mother and the other women. Sometimes we chase the water goannas right under the water or dig the sand goannas out of their holes. Once, we found a big goanna by the road on the way to the fishing hole. It belonged to my Auntie Cleo, even though someone else killed it. Auntie cooked the goanna and shared it because she saw it first.

The women get a lot of bush-tucker from the billabongs. They gather the stems and seed pods from the waterlily plants, or collect freshwater mussels and crayfish. We all learn how to find things to eat by going out in the bush with our families.

At the end of the Wet Season we can pick all kinds of fruit, like white currants and black plums. The green plums are ready to eat just before the rains come. We pick up the ripe plums from around the tree and then throw sticks to knock more plums off the branches.

Wild honey is one of the best kinds of bush-tucker. We call it 'sugarbag'. The bees which make the honey look like little black flies. You have to follow them back to their tree to find the honey. They don't even sting you when you cut into the tree to open up their hive. We eat the honey mixed with the yellow pollen.

We collect lots of other useful things from the bush. There are soap berries for washing your hands and bushes for making brooms. We use palm leaves for weaving baskets and bags, or different clays and rocks for making paints. Some of the old people can make medicines from plants. They can cure headaches, colds, cuts and sores.

One of the houses at the Camp is used as a Government Clinic. Mary, the Health Worker, keeps the medicines in the clinic. We can see her whenever we want.

If someone is very ill, they call the Flying Doctor by radio. Then the doctor will take them to hospital. The doctor flies out to Hodgson Downs every six weeks, to treat sick people at home. The airstrip is six kilometres away and someone has to go and bring the doctor to the Camp.

Once, my Auntie Rosie was very ill during the Wet Season. The roads were flooded and no-one could fetch the doctor from the airstrip. Auntie Rosie had to swim two streams and walk a long way through the mud to meet the plane. The doctor took her to the hospital in Katherine. When she was better, Auntie Rosie came back to Minyerri.

There are lots of other children to play with at the Camp. I like to play marbles, softball, basketball and three-can. To play three-can, you have to knock over a pile of cans with a ball. You win the game if you can stand the three cans back on top of each other before anyone hits you with the ball.

After school, we often go swimming in the billabong. Sometimes we go to the waterhole at Bella Glen, about 15 kilometres away.

At the beginning of the Wet Season, the weather is very hot. After the first rains, the rivers and streams fill with water. Then we can cool off in the waterfalls, or slide down the rocks. In the Dry Season we can swim in the waterholes. There's clay in the riverbanks for making models and plenty of mud to slide on, or paint yourself with.

A lot of people like travelling around to work or visit relatives. I liked seeing Darwin and Batchelor, but it's always good to be back in your own country.

Glossary

Many of the words in this book have special meanings for Aboriginal people. This glossary will help you to understand some of these words.

Ceremonies: Religious rituals, often with singing and dancing. Ceremonies are usually held at special dreaming places. Aborigines believe that they can get in touch with the Dreamtime spirits during ceremonies. They are also important for passing down tribal law.

Dreaming: This is an English word for an Aboriginal belief. It doesn't mean the dreaming you do when you go to sleep. It means the religious feelings and laws which an Aborigine has about his country and about the spirits who created the world.

Dreaming places: Special places where events happened during the Dreamtime, especially where the Dreamtime spirits sank back into the earth. According to Aboriginal belief, the spirits still remain there.

Dreamtime: The time when the world was created. Spirits walked over the land and made the countryside, plants, animals and people.

Dreamtime spirits: The creatures who created the world during the Dreamtime. These spirits could take the shape of people, animals or other things. After the Dreamtime, they sank back into the earth.

Skin groups: Most traditional Aborigines belong to a skin group. A person's skin group would depend on their mother's skin group. Their mother, father, children, in-laws and grandparents would usually be in different skin groups. Each skin group follows rules about who they should marry, which people to look after and many other things. Skin groups are important because they are a way of making all Aborigines related to each other, like a big family.